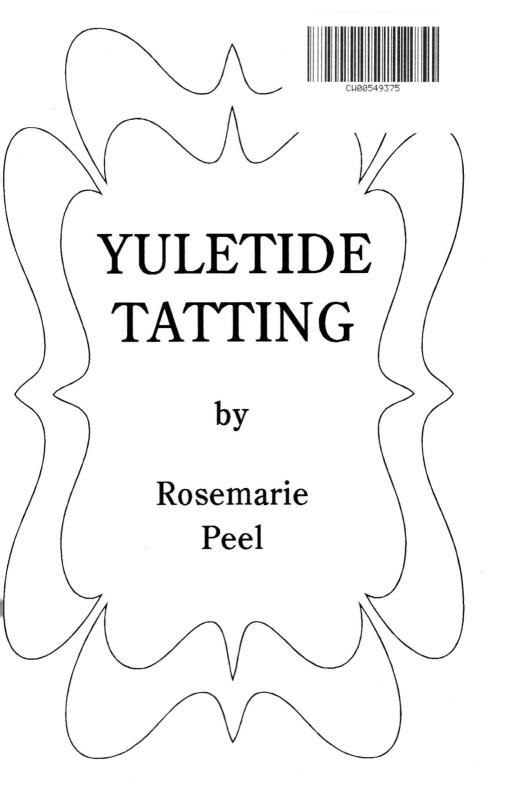

YULETIDE TATTING

by

Rosemarie Peel

Contents

Other books in this series:
TAT FIVE
BEAD TATTING

ISBN 1 874688 01 X

Printed in England by
Printhaus graphique
Northampton.

First published in September 1992 by
Lacet Publications
29, St Nicolas Park Drive, Nuneaton, CV11 6DL

Introduction

'YULETIDE TATTING' is for all tatters who know how to make the double stitch in both rings and chains, how to reverse work, how to join and make a lock join.

Many of my patterns are worked all in one. When I am designing I like the tatting to flow continuously from beginning to end. I'm sure the origins of this come from my Dad, an expert at line drawings, who would amuse me as a child by drawing pictures without taking his pencil off the paper.

The tatter can use the ideas from this book to decorate many festive items: for example your Christmas tree, stockings, gift tags, cards, crackers, and the cake. So, happy tatting to you all, and -

Pinning out

Most patterns in this book make tatting that looks like an object or a word: so the finished work has to be set in position. Picots may need to be pointed to suggest frost or fingers or antlers etc. Similarly the rings may need to be held at a certain angle.

On completion, wet the tatting. If it needs more than a quick handwash boil it in a pan over the stove in pure soap and water for 20 minutes.

The wet tatting is straightened out and all the worked-in and sewn-in ends are trimmed off. It is then pinned out precisely on a board (cork or polystyrene) which does not release its colour. On the 'Noel' above I have illustrated with black dots where to put 12 pins in order to give the word its shape. The pattern for Noel is on page 6.

If your tatting is the same size as the line drawings in the book take a tracing of them and pin your work out on that.

When the tatting is dry its shape is set and it is ready for mounting or sewing onto its backing.

Before being hung on a Christmas tree the Bell and the Snowflakes will need extra stiffening. Dip them in sugar water before pinning them out. To make the sugar water simmer one cup of sugar with one cup of water until dissolved.

Abbreviations

TATTING TERM and ABBREVIATION		EXPLANATION	DIAGRAM SYMBOLS
Double stitch	1, ds	The number denotes the quantity. Made up of two halves, plain and purl.	
Picot	-	Comes between whole ds. - (regular) - - (long)	
Chain	Ch	A number of ds. made with the ball thread and sitting on the shuttle thread.	
Ring	R	A number of ds. made using shuttle thread only.	
Close ring	close	Work continues from this close up point on the ring.	
Reverse work	RW	The ring is tipped upside down before the next chain is made. Another RW tips it back.	
Shuttle	Sh	see page 5 for full details.	
Ball			
Join	+	A join is made to the appropriate free picot followed by a purl. This counts as the next ds.	
Lock join	LJ	Make this join with the shuttle thread in use at the time.	
Josephine knot	JK	see the top of page 6.	
Bead	- b + b	see the bottom of page 22.	

Using two shuttles

By having the ball thread on a second shuttle the tatting can be more versatile. It allows rings to be made with the thread which normally makes the double stitches on a chain or a chain can change direction. (Fig.1)

Unless you are positive about how much thread is needed always wind the shuttle full. Turn the shuttle and not the thread to minimise extra twist on the thread. Do not cut the wound shuttle from the ball of thread if the tatting is to be in one colour. To wind a second shuttle, take four armslengths of thread from the ball after winding the first shuttle, cut, and wind onto the second shuttle until the shuttles are about 50cm apart.

Five ways to prepare to tat are:-

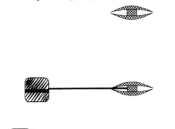

1) Shuttle thread only -
   for a pattern made up entirely of rings. Measure with a gauge any thread which has to be left between one ring and the next.

2) Ball and shuttle thread continuous -
   for tatting with basic rings and chains in one colour.

3) Ball and shuttle thread joined -
   for the basic tatting in two colours. The rings will be the colour on the shuttle and the chains the colour of the ball. Tie the ball and shuttle threads together in a reef knot and get rid of the ends within their own colour.

4) Two shuttles continuous -
   for one colour tatting.

5) Two shuttles joined -
   for two colour tatting. Tie the two shuttle threads together in a reef knot as in 3 above.

The shuttle requirements for all the patterns in this book are indicated by the symbols above. If two shuttles are used name them shuttle one (Sh1) and shuttle two (Sh2). It helps if they are a different colour or make. I always have my favourite shuttle as shuttle one.

Fig.1 Examples of the use of two shuttles -

Sh1: Ch 5, RW,
Sh2: Ch 5.

Sh1: Ch 3
Sh2: R 10 close,
Sh1: Ch 5
Sh2: R 10 close
Sh1: Ch 3

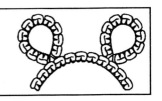

With the abbreviations Sh1 and Sh2 the written instructions indicate which shuttle to use. If there is no mention of a shuttle for a long time this just means there has been no change.

Josephine knots

A Josephine knot is formed in exactly the same way as a ring but using just one half of the double stitch. It doesn't matter whether all plain or all purl stitches are used because the reverse sides of plain stitches are the same as purl stitches and vice versa. Therefore I use the purl (the second half of the ds) because it is quicker to make.

The plain and the purl stitches complement each other in the double stitch. As the Josephine knot is made up of only purl stitches it is inclined to be unstable and needs to be closed up with care. Flatten all its stitches under your finger and thumb while pulling up the ring.

JK is the abbreviation for a Josephine Knot and the number after it denotes the number of purls to make. The symbol used for the JK is a circle divided into segments equal to the number of half stitches to be made. Below (enlarged) are the abbreviations and symbols for Josephine knots containing 8, 10 and 12 half stitches respectively.

JK 8    JK 10    JK 12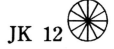

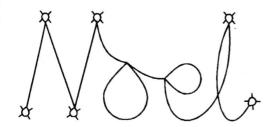

The working diagram for Noel is on page 3.

Start at the first ring at the bottom of the letter 'N'
Sh1: R 1 - 1 - 1 - 1 - 1 close, RW, Ch 15, RW,
Make sure the next 2 chains are the same length as this last one.
R 1 - 1 - 1 - 1 - 1 close, Ch 15, RW, R 1 - 1 - 1 - 1 - 1 close,
Sh2: Ch 15, RW, R 1 - 1 - 1 - 1 - 1 close, RW, Ch 10,
Sh1: R 30 close,
Sh2: Ch 7, RW, R 20 close, RW, Ch 35,
Sh1: R 1 - 1 - 1 - 1 - 1 close
Sh2: Ch 15, sandwich the chain before this one between the two threads (Sh2 thread on top and Sh1 thread underneath). Continue the chain on the other side.
Ch 5, RW, R 1 - 1 - 1 - 1 - 1 close. Cut, tie and sew in ends.

Cobweb snowflake

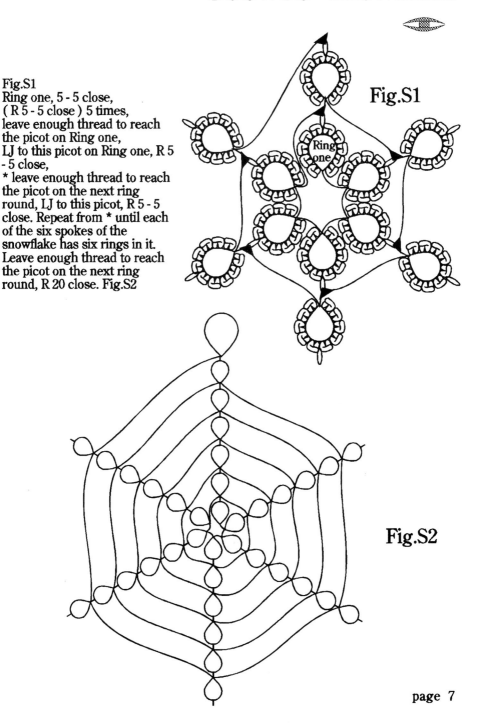

Fig.S1
Ring one, 5 - 5 close,
(R 5 - 5 close) 5 times,
leave enough thread to reach
the picot on Ring one,
LJ to this picot on Ring one, R 5
- 5 close,
* leave enough thread to reach
the picot on the next ring
round, LJ to this picot, R 5 - 5
close. Repeat from * until each
of the six spokes of the
snowflake has six rings in it.
Leave enough thread to reach
the picot on the next ring
round, R 20 close. Fig.S2

Fig.S1

Ring
one

Fig.S2

Icy snowflake

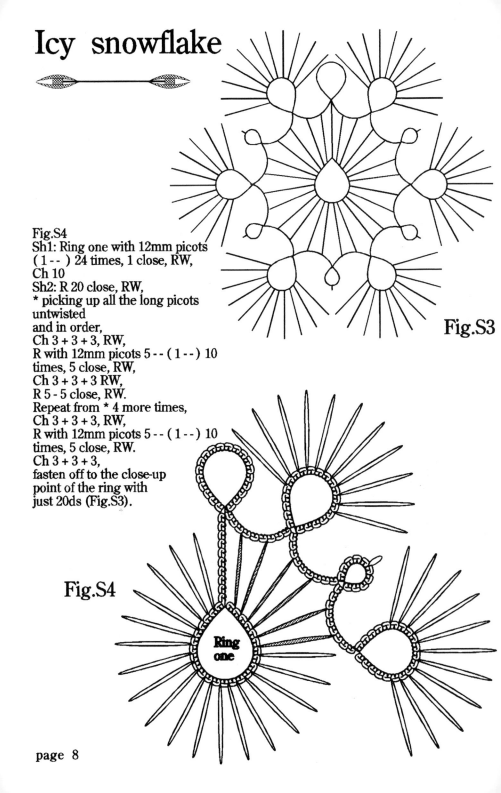

Fig.S4
Sh1: Ring one with 12mm picots
(1 --) 24 times, 1 close, RW,
Ch 10
Sh2: R 20 close, RW,
* picking up all the long picots
untwisted
and in order,
Ch 3 + 3 + 3, RW,
R with 12mm picots 5 -- (1 --) 10
times, 5 close, RW,
Ch 3 + 3 + 3 RW,
R 5 - 5 close, RW.
Repeat from * 4 more times,
Ch 3 + 3 + 3, RW,
R with 12mm picots 5 -- (1 --) 10
times, 5 close, RW.
Ch 3 + 3 + 3,
fasten off to the close-up
point of the ring with
just 20ds (Fig.S3).

Fig.S3

Fig.S4

Ring
one

Soft snowflake

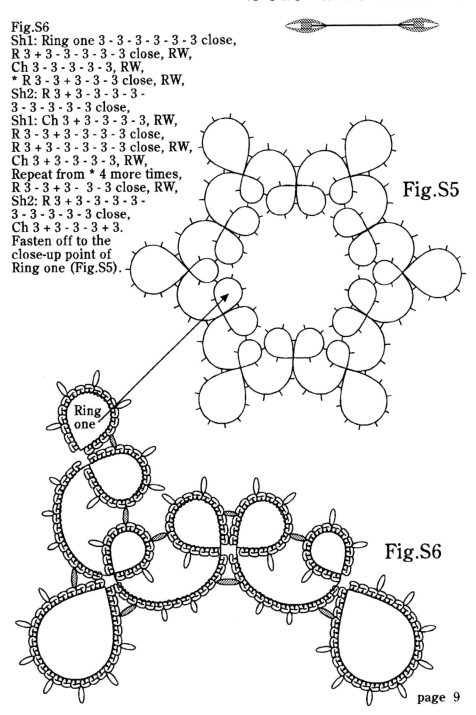

Fig.S6
Sh1: Ring one 3 - 3 - 3 - 3 - 3 - 3 close,
R 3 + 3 - 3 - 3 - 3 - 3 close, RW,
Ch 3 - 3 - 3 - 3 - 3, RW,
* R 3 - 3 + 3 - 3 - 3 close, RW,
Sh2: R 3 + 3 - 3 - 3 - 3 -
3 - 3 - 3 - 3 - 3 close,
Sh1: Ch 3 + 3 - 3 - 3 - 3, RW,
R 3 - 3 + 3 - 3 - 3 - 3 close,
R 3 + 3 - 3 - 3 - 3 - 3 close, RW,
Ch 3 + 3 - 3 - 3 - 3, RW,
Repeat from * 4 more times,
R 3 - 3 + 3 - 3 - 3 close, RW,
Sh2: R 3 + 3 - 3 - 3 - 3 -
3 - 3 - 3 - 3 - 3 close,
Ch 3 + 3 - 3 - 3 + 3.
Fasten off to the
close-up point of
Ring one (Fig.S5).

Fig.S5

Ring
one

Fig.S6

Large snowflake

The working diagram on this page shows one spoke of the snowflake. The line drawing on the opposite page illustrates the whole of it.

Fig.S7 Ring one 2 - 2 - 2 - 2 - 2 - 2 - 2 - 2 - 8 - 8 close, RW,
Ch 2 - 2 - 2 - 2 - 2 - 2 - 2 - 2, RW,
* R 7 + 7 - 7 - 7 close, RW,
Ch 2 - 2 - 2 - 2 - 2 - 2 - 2, RW,
R 6 + 6 - 6 - 6 close, RW,
Ch 2 - 2 - 2 - 2 - 2 - 2, RW,
R 5 + 5 - 5 - 5 close, RW,
Ch 2 - 2 - 2 - 2 - 2, RW,
R 4 + 4 - 4 - 4 close, RW,
Ch 2 - 2 - 2 - 2, RW,
R 3 + 3 - 3 - 3 close, RW,
Ch 2 - 2 - 2, RW,
R 2 + 2 - 2 - 2 close, RW,
Ch 2 - 2 - 2 - 2 - 2 - 2 - 2,
LJ to the second picot of the last ring.
The following six chains LJ to the next free picot on each of the rings, up to the last picot on the largest ring.
Ch 2 - 2 - 2, LJ,
Ch 2 - 2 - 2 - 2, LJ,
Ch 2 - 2 - 2 - 2 - 2, LJ,
Ch 2 - 2 - 2 - 2 - 2 - 2, LJ,
Ch 2 - 2 - 2 - 2 - 2 - 2 - 2, LJ,
Ch 2 - 2 - 2 - 2 - 2 - 2 - 2 - 2, LJ,
Ch 2 + 2, RW,
R 4 + 4 - 4 - 4 - 4, RW,
Ch 2 - 2, RW,
joining to the last picot on the last ring
R 2 - 2 + 2 - 2 - 2 - 2 - 2 - 2 - 8 - 8 close, RW,
joining to the picot on the last chain
Ch 2 + 2 - 2 - 2 - 2 - 2 - 2 - 2, RW,
repeat from * until six spokes have been made (Fig.S8). The last small inner ring and chain are
R 4 + 4 - 4 - 4 + 4 close, RW,
Ch 2 + 2, fasten off to the close-up point of Ring one.

Ring one

To cover a bauble

Worked in No.20 crochet cotton the Large snowflake is approximately 20cm in diameter and will fit round a bauble 6cm in diameter. Much finer thread would make the snowflake the size in Fig.S8.

Put the centre of the snowflake over the hanging loop of a bauble (Fig.S9), gather up the six spokes at the bottom with matching thread, tie firmly and trim. The snowflake can be easily removed for laundering by cutting away this thread.

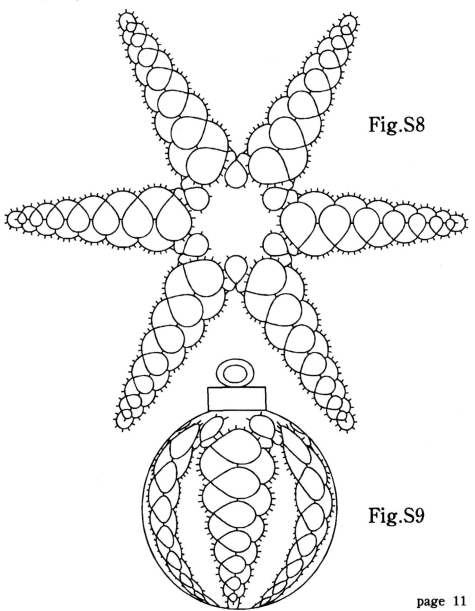

Fig.S8

Fig.S9

Angel

Materials

A doll, 8cm high, from a doll's house.
The dress pattern below cut from some fabric of handkerchief thickness.
Coats Mercer crochet cotton No 40. The line drawings with this pattern show the approximate size of the tatting when this thread is used.

Three pieces of tatting are to be made to trim the angel:-
1) Edging for the bottom of the dress.
2) Wings
3) Halo

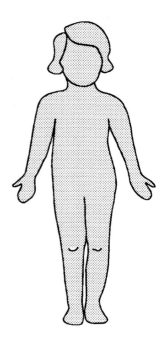

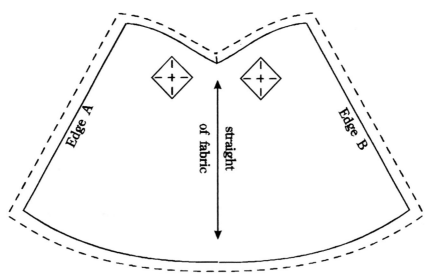

DRESS PATTERN
Cut along the dotted lines and fold along the solid lines.
The folded seams can be held down with a small running stitch.
There is no back seam, just lay Edge A over Edge B at the back of the doll.

1) Edging for the bottom of the dress

With ball and shuttle thread:-
Ring one 6 - 3 - 3 close,
R 3 - 3 - 6 close, RW,
* Ch 2 - 2 - 2 - 2 - 2 - 2 - 2 - 2 - 2 - 2, RW,
R 6 + 3 - 3 close, R 3 - 3 - 6 close, RW,
Repeat from * 7 more times.
Sew onto the bottom of the dress by
picking up the free picots on the rings.

2) Wings

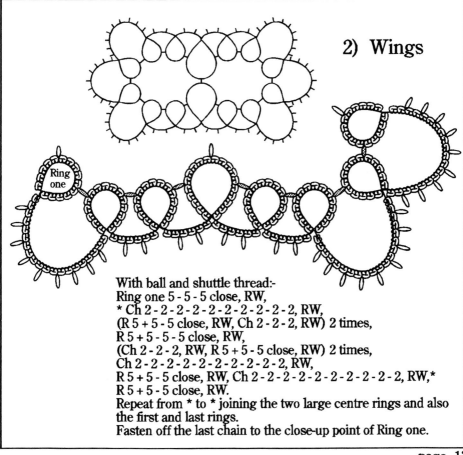

With ball and shuttle thread:-
Ring one 5 - 5 - 5 close, RW,
* Ch 2 - 2 - 2 - 2 - 2 - 2 - 2 - 2 - 2 - 2, RW,
(R 5 + 5 - 5 close, RW, Ch 2 - 2 - 2, RW) 2 times,
R 5 + 5 - 5 - 5 close, RW,
(Ch 2 - 2 - 2, RW, R 5 + 5 - 5 close, RW) 2 times,
Ch 2 - 2 - 2 - 2 - 2 - 2 - 2 - 2 - 2 - 2, RW,
R 5 + 5 - 5 close, RW, Ch 2 - 2 - 2 - 2 - 2 - 2 - 2 - 2 - 2 - 2, RW,*
R 5 + 5 - 5 close, RW.
Repeat from * to * joining the two large centre rings and also
the first and last rings.
Fasten off the last chain to the close-up point of Ring one.

3) Halo

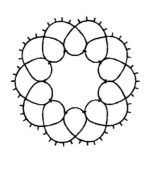

With ball and shuttle thread:-
Ring one 5 - 5 - 5 close, RW,
* Ch 2 - 2 - 2 - 2 - 2 - 2, RW,
R 5 + 5 - 5 close, RW,
Repeat from * 7 more times.
Ch 2 - 2 - 2 - 2 - 2 - 2, RW,
R 5 + 5 + 5 close, RW,
Ch 2 - 2 - 2 - 2 - 2 - 2.
Fasten off to the close-up
point of Ring one.

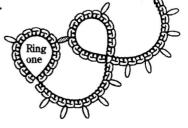

To dress the Angel

Take the dress with the tatted edging attached and slip it on over the doll's arms. Overlap the two back edges of the dress and sew on the wings through both layers. The wings only need to be sewn on by the join of their two large central rings.

Place the halo on the head of the doll.

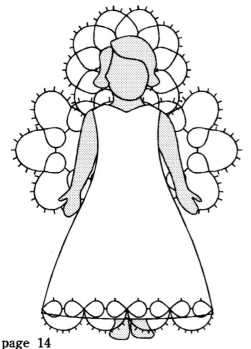

3D bell

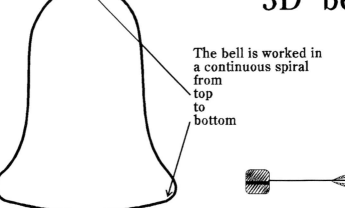

The bell is worked in
a continuous spiral
from
top
to
bottom

To make a bell about 6cm high use No 20
crochet cotton.
Start with the ring at the top of the bell. Fig.B1.
Top Ring 2 - 2 - 2 - 2 - 2 - 2 - 2 - 2 - 2 - 2 close.

RW, (Ch 2 - 2 - 2 - 2, miss 1 picot LJ to the next
picot) 13 times.
Fig.B2 shows how these chains fit round the
ring and then on top of each other.

Fig.B1

Fig.B2

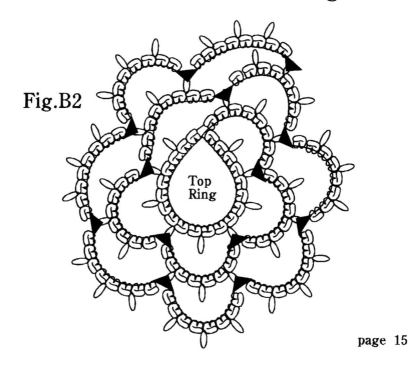

To make the bell shape the tatting starts to close in and it is not possible to show all the stitches. Fig.B3 converts Fig.B2 so that just the first ring and chain are shown in detail followed by lines representing the other 12 chains and their picots.

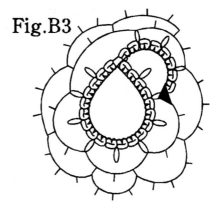

Fig.B3

Fig.B4 contains Fig.B3 and continues again with the stitches illustrated in full the first time they are worked, then the repeats are represented by lines.
(Ch 3 - 3 - 3 - 3 miss 2 picots LJ to the next picot) 15 times,
Ch 3 - 3 - 3 - 3 miss 1 picot LJ to the next picot,
(Ch 3 - 3 - 3 - 3, RW,
R 5 miss one picot join to next picot 5 close,
R 5 join to next picot 5 close, RW) 9 times.

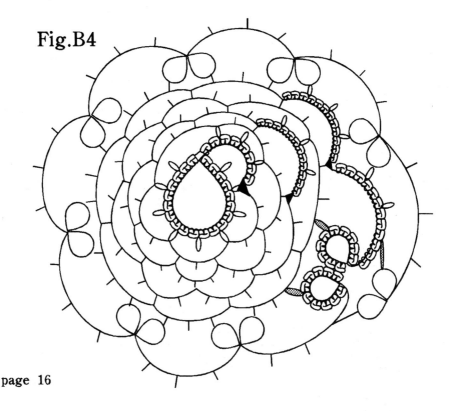

Fig.B4

Fig.B5 illustrates in line form the positions of all the pairs of rings in the
ell and the final round of chains. The rings are all the same size but the
hains between them vary in length so the written instructions must be
llowed carefully.

Fig.B5

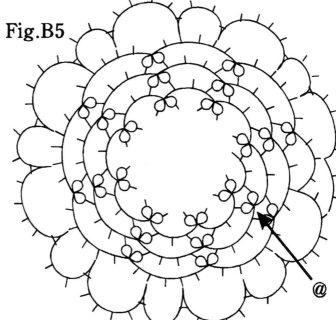

or the finishing
uch the bell
eds a clanger.
art a chain on a
t bell (from a
t shop) then
d a ring. Attach
e two ends
und the top of
e bell with the
ng above and
e chain and
anger inside.

@

ontinue the spiral (from pointer on Fig.B5):-
(Ch 3 - 3 - 3 - 3 - 3, RW, R 5 miss 1 picot and join to next picot 5 close,
5 join to next picot 5 close, RW) 8 times.
Ch 3 - 3 - 3 - 3 - 3 - 3, RW, R 5 miss 2 picots and join to next picot 5 close,
5 join to next picot 5 close, RW) 7 times.
h 3 - 3 - 3 - 3, miss 1 picot
J to the next picot,
h 3 - 3 - 3 - 3 - 3 - 3 - 3, miss 2 picots
J to the next picot,
Ch 3 + 3 - 3 - 3 - 3, miss 1 picot
J to the next picot,
h 3 + 3 - 3 - 3 - 3 - 3 - 3, miss 2 picots
J to the next picot) 6 times.
ig.B6 illustrates one repeat.
h 3 + 3 - 3 - 3 - 3, miss 1 picot
J to the next picot,
h 3 + 3 - 3 - 3 - 3 - 3, miss 2 picots
J to the next picot,
h 3 - 3 - 3, miss 2 picots,
sten off to the next picot and sew in ends.

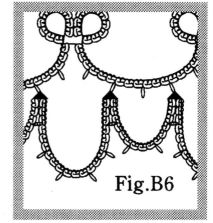

Fig.B6

On completion stiffen the bell with sugar water (page 3) and pin out on an
bject which will give it the right shape. I use a small polythene bag rolled up
nd placed on the top of a shampoo bottle top. The bell is pinned down over
ese by all the picots round the bottom edge.

Christmas cake frill

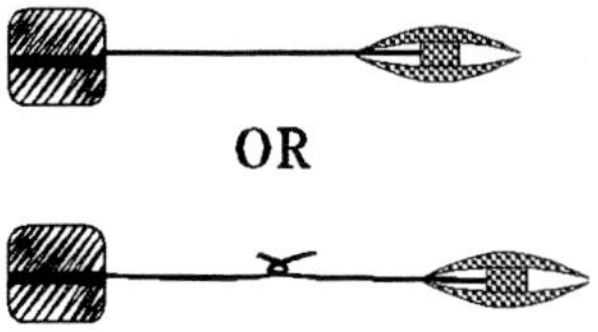

Materials
No.20 crochet cotton.
Ribbon 36mm wide.

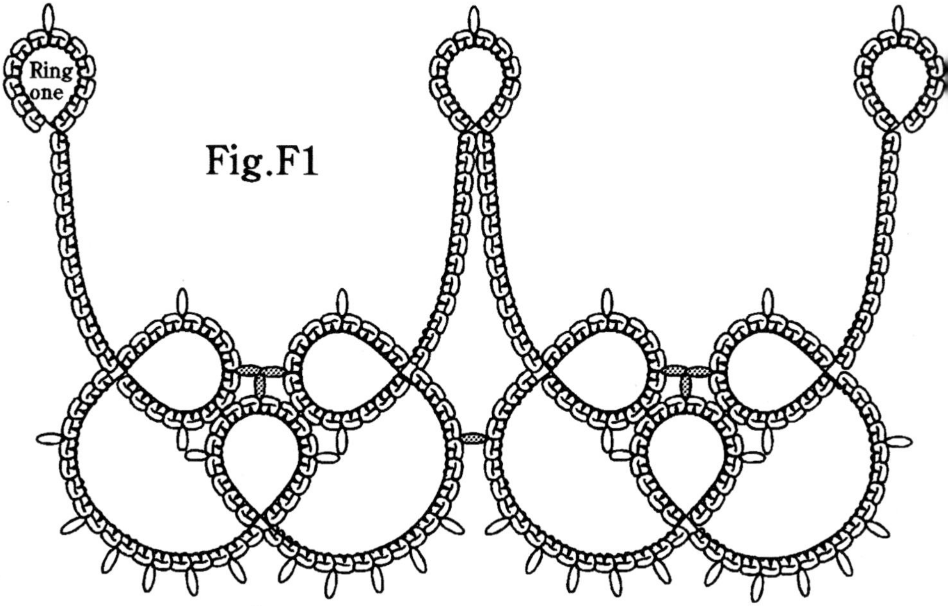

OR

Fig.F1

Ring one

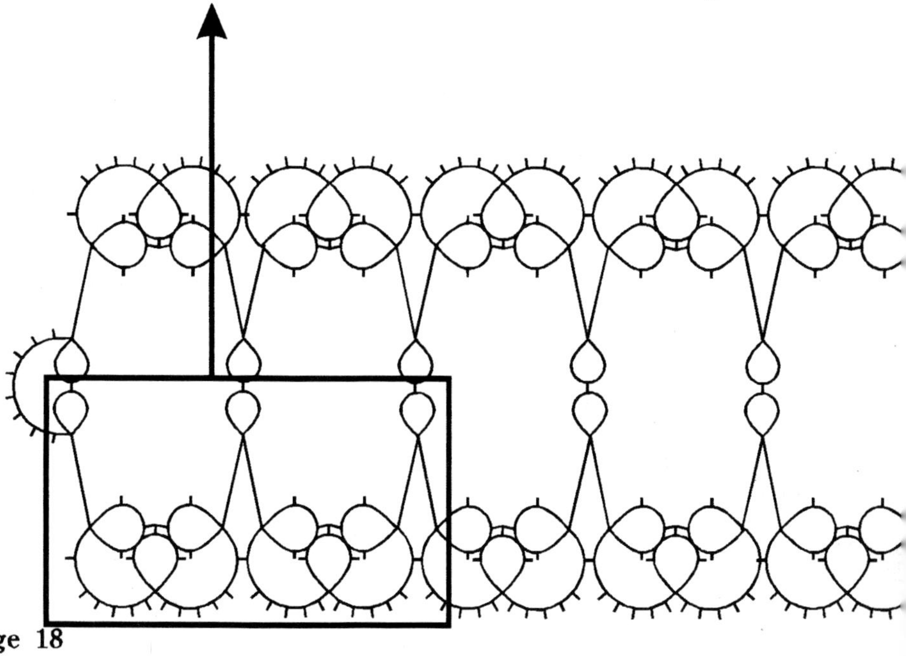

LOWER SIDE Fig.F1
Ring one 6 - 6 close, RW,
Ch 12, RW,
R 4 - 4 - 4 - 4 close, RW,
Ch 4 - 4 - 2 - 2 - 2 - 2 - 2, RW,
R, 4 - 4 + 4 - 4 close, RW.
Ch 2 - 2 - 2 - 2 - 2 - 4 - 4, RW,
R 4 - 4 + 4 - 4 close, RW,
Ch 12, RW,
R 6 - 6 close, RW,
* Ch 12, RW,
R 4 - 4 - 4 - 4 close, RW,
Ch 4 + 4 - 2 - 2 - 2 - 2 - 2, RW,
R 4 - 4 + 4 - 4 close, RW,
Ch 2 - 2 - 2 - 2 - 2 - 4 - 4, RW,
R 4 - 4 + 4 - 4 close, RW,
Ch 12, RW,
R 6 - 6 close, RW,
Repeat from * for the length required. Make an
odd number of centre rings so that both ends of
the frill will show on the same side of the ribbon.

END OF FRILL (Fig.F2)
Ch 2 - 2 - 2 - 2 - 2 - 2 - 2 - 2 - 2, RW,
TOP SIDE
R 6 + 6 close, RW,
Now repeat again from * joining the
corresponding centre rings (Fig.F3).
Make as many repeats as are needed to cover the
lower half, finishing with a central joined ring,
RW, Ch 2 - 2 - 2 - 2 - 2 - 2 - 2 - 2 - 2.

Fasten off to the close-up point of Ring one.
Thread the ribbon in and out through the tatting.

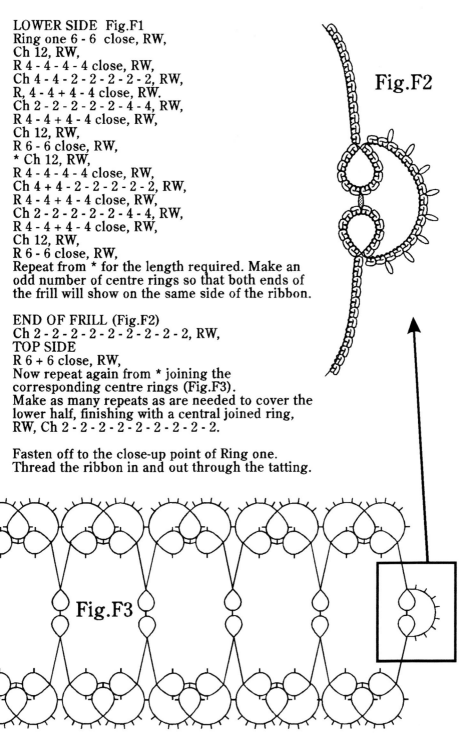

Fig.F2

Fig.F3

Mr Frostie

Worked in No.20 crochet cotton, Mr Frostie will be approximately the size illustrated in Fig.M3. Mr Frostie is made completely with basic rings and chains so just ball and shuttle threads are used throughout. His face (Fig.M1) and inner body (Fig.M2) are tatted separately first. The rest of his body outline is then worked onto these two pieces (Fig.M3).

See 'Pinning out' on page 3

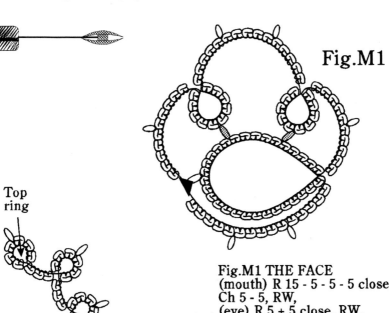

Fig.M1

Top ring

Fig.M2

Fig.M1 THE FACE
(mouth) R 15 - 5 - 5 - 5 close, RW,
Ch 5 - 5, RW,
(eye) R 5 + 5 close, RW,
Ch 5 - 5 - 5, RW,
(eye) R 5 + 5 close, RW, Ch 5 - 5, RW,
LJ to picot at end of mouth,
Ch 5 - 5 - 5, fasten off to the close-up point of the mouth ring.
On Fig.M3 the face is shown in grey to identify it.

Fig.M2 THE INNER BODY
Top ring:- R 3 - 3 close, RW,
(Ch 3, RW, R 3 - 3, RW,) 2 times,
(Ch 6 - 6, RW, R 3 - 3, RW,) 2 times.
On Fig.M3 the inner body is shown in grey and its rings are filled in to identify them.

Fig.M3 THE BODY OUTLINE

Start at the ring marked @ and work in the direction of the head.

R 3 - - 3 close, RW, Ch 6 - 6, RW, R 3 - - 3 close, (the next two rings join to this last one) RW,

joining to the top ring on the inner body,Ch 6 - 6 + 6, RW, R 3 + 3 close, RW,

joining to a picot on the chin,Ch 3 + 3, RW, R 3 + 3 close, RW,

the next nine chains join either between the chains round the face or to the picots on those chains.

Ch 3 + 3, RW, R 3 - - 3 close, RW) 8 times,

Ch 3 + 6 + 6, joining to the face then the inner body, RW, R 3 + 3 close RW.

From here follow the line drawing in Fig.M3 to check where joins are made.

All future chains are 6 - (or +) 6, RW.

All rings are 3 - - (or +) 3 close, RW, except the hands and feet.

The first hand is R 5 - - 4 - - 1 - - 1 - - 1 - - 9, RW,

Both feet are R 15 - - 10 - 5 close, RW,

The second hand is

9 - - 1 - - 1 - - 1 - - 4 - - 5 close, RW.

Ch 6 + 6, fasten off to the close up point of the ring marked @.

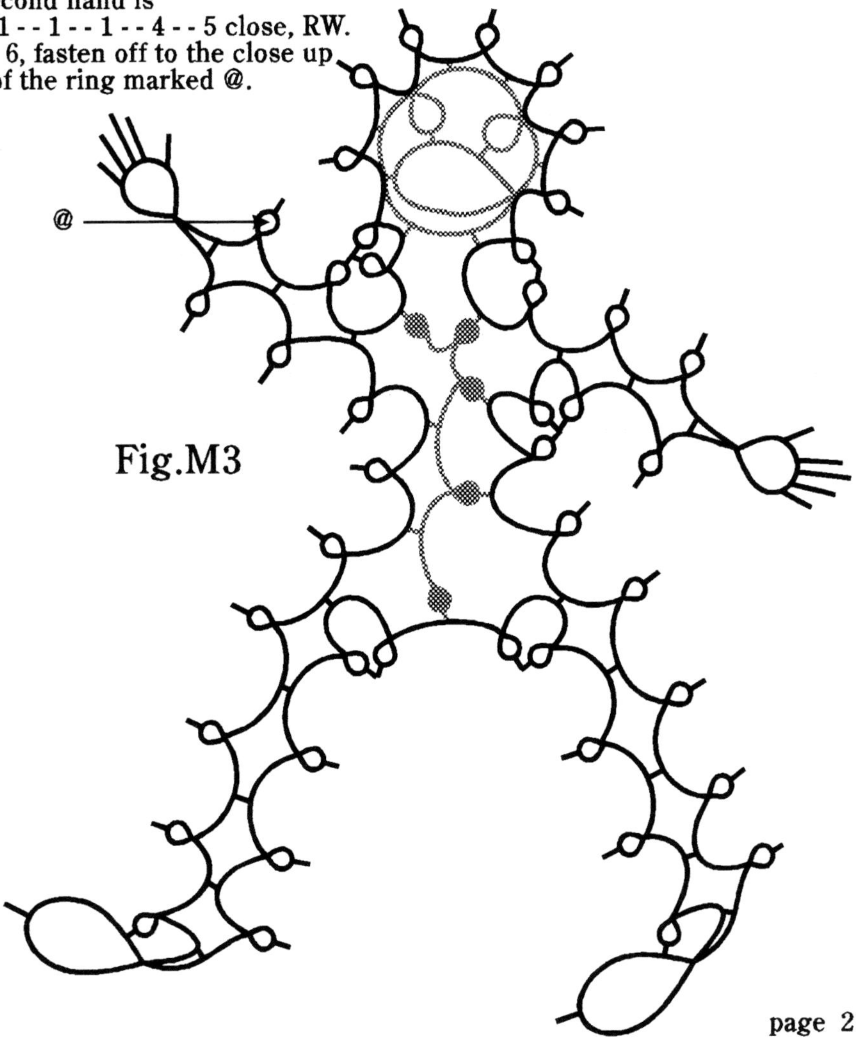

Fig.M3

@

Decorated Tree

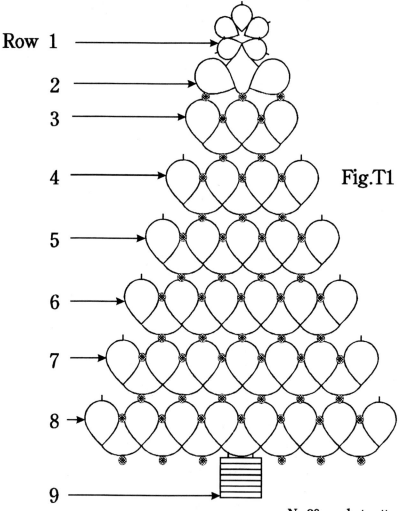

Row 1

2

3

4   Fig.T1

5

6

7

8

9

Suggested materials -
(to give the approx. size shown above)

No.20 crochet cotton in white for the star (Row 1), green for the tree (Rows 2 to 8) brown for the tub (Row 9). 56 x 3mm beads.

Start each row with the ring which is arrowed on Fig.T1.
Make all picots 3 mm long to accomodate the beads.

Beads are added on rows 3 to 8 in two ways:-
    + b = put a bead on a fine hook, put the hook into the picot to be
           joined, pass the bead along from hook to picot then complete
           the join as normal.
    - b = slide a bead already on the thread into the place of a picot.

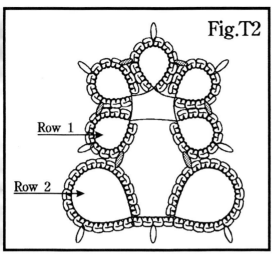

Fig.T2
Row 1 THE STAR
R 3 - 3 - 3 - 3 close,
(R 3 + 3 - 3 - 3 close) 4 times,
cut and tie the ends.
If the tree is going to be mounted
then all the ends can be sewn
through the backing.

Rewind the shuttle from the ball
every row. Each row will take a
little more thread.
Row 2 THE TREE
R 5 - 10 + 5 close, RW,
Ch 2 - 2, RW,
R 5 + 10 - 5 close,
cut and tie the ends.

Fig.T3 Row 3, R 10 + b 5 - 5 close, RW, Ch 5 - 5, RW, R 5 + b 5 + b 5 - 5 close, RW,
Ch 5 - 5 , RW, R 5 + b 5 + b 10 close, cut and tie ends.
Row 4, R 10 - 5 - 5 close, RW, Ch 5 - 5, RW, (R 5 + b 5 + b 5 - 5 close, RW,
Ch 5 - 5, RW) 2 times, R 5 + b 5 - 10 close, cut and tie ends.
Rows 5, 6 and 7, as row 4 but each with one more ring and chain repeat.

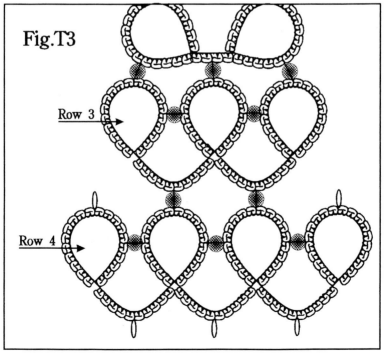

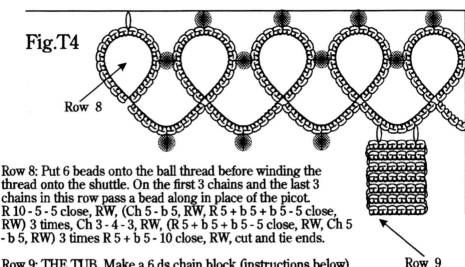

Fig.T4

Row 8

Row 9

Row 8: Put 6 beads onto the ball thread before winding the thread onto the shuttle. On the first 3 chains and the last 3 chains in this row pass a bead along in place of the picot. R 10 - 5 - 5 close, RW, (Ch 5 - b 5, RW, R 5 + b 5 + b 5 - 5 close, RW) 3 times, Ch 3 - 4 - 3, RW, (R 5 + b 5 + b 5 - 5 close, RW, Ch 5 - b 5, RW) 3 times R 5 + b 5 - 10 close, RW, cut and tie ends.

Row 9: THE TUB. Make a 6 ds chain block (instructions below) with 6 rows. Make a 7th row joining it to the centre chain at the bottom of the tree, Ch 1 + 4 + 1, LJ, cut and tie ends.

A 6ds Chain Block

With ball and shuttle thread:-
a) Make 6ds starting on a paperclip to make a picot.
b) Turn the work sideways and do a reverse stitch (this is the first half of the ds pulled up like a single knot so that the ball and shuttle threads change position).
c) Make a small picot and mark it with a different coloured thread. Ch 6, LJ to the picot at the beginning of the previous row removing paperclip or marker thread.
Repeat b) and c) for the number of rows required.

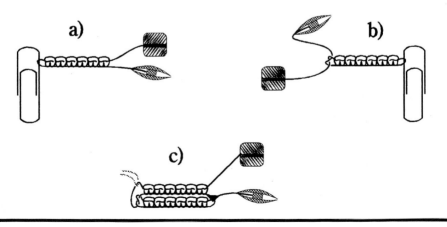

a)

b)

c)

Lighted candle in candlestick

Worked in No.20 crochet cotton or similar the tatting will be approximately the size illustrated here: ideal for a bookmark.
Two shuttles are needed as well as a paperclip and a 16mm gauge.

The instructions (pp 25/27) work up the left hand side then down the right hand side of the motif.

Fig.C1 Sh1: Ring one 10 close, RW, Ch 10 - 10,
Sh2: R 6 - 3 - 3 close, RW,
(Ch 8, RW, R 3 + 3 - 3 - 3 close, RW,) 6 times.
Ch 8, RW, R 3 + 3 - 6 close, RW.

Fig.C2 Ch 8 - 4, loop Sh2 thread over a paperclip,
continue Ch 4 + 15, loop Sh2 thread over
the paperclip again, continue Ch 10,

Fig.C3 Sh1: JK 10, (see page 6) RW, Ch 10,
Sh2: R 6 + (join to last loop put on paperclip) 6 - 6
close,
(Sh1: Ch 5 - - make an extra long picot using a
16mm gauge) 7 times.
Remove gauge, continue Ch 5, RW.

Fig.C4 R 2 close, RW, Ch 6, RW,
R 12 close, turn this ring so Sh1 thread lies to the
left ready for the next ring.
Large outer ring (made over the small ring)
15 - 15 close, RW,
Ch 6, RW, R 2 close, RW.

The next chain makes the other side of the candle.
Pick up the long picots and give them two twists
before completing each of the seven joins.
Ch 5 + 5 + 5 + 5 + 5 + 5 + 5 + 5,

Fig.C5 Sh2: R 6 + 6 - 6 close, Sh1: Ch 10, RW,
make sure the last chain (50 ds in all) is the same
as the other side.
JK 10,
Sh2: Ch 10, LJ to free picot on last ring,
Ch 15 - 4, LJ to remaining loop on paperclip,
Ch 4 + 8, LJ to the free picot on the next ring,
(Ch 8, LJ to the free picot on the next ring) 7 times.

Fig.C6, RW. Sh1: Ch 10 - 10, RW, R 10 close,
Sh2: Ch 15, LJ, Ch 20, LJ, Ch 15,
fasten off to the close-up point of Ring one.

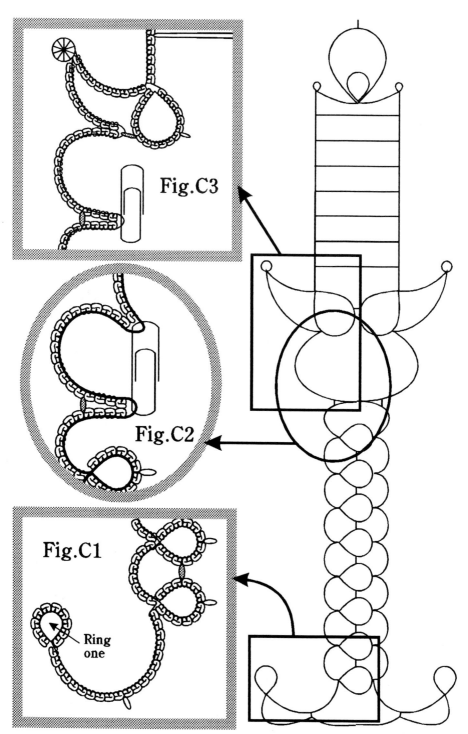

Fig.C3

Fig.C2

Fig.C1

Ring one

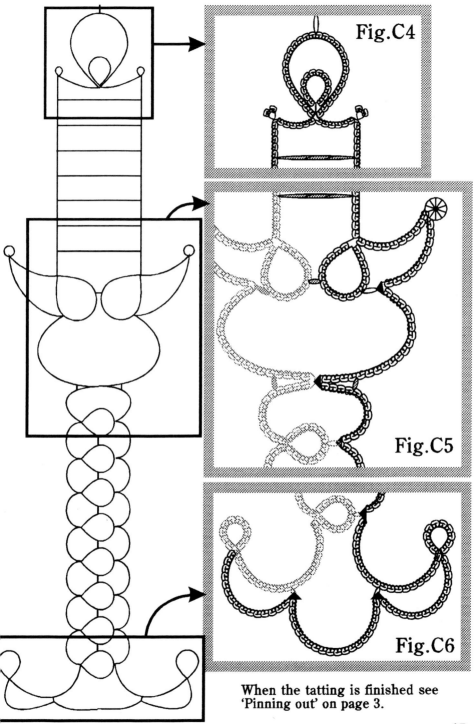

Fig.C4

Fig.C5

Fig.C6

When the tatting is finished see
'Pinning out' on page 3.

Rudolph reindeer edging

Materials

No.20 crochet cotton
(Fig.R1 is approx. size)
4mm red bead per head
4mm & 8mm gauges

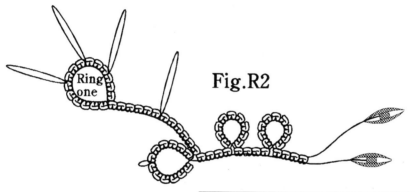

Fig.R1

Use an 8mm gauge for all picots on the antlers.
Fig.R2 Sh1: Ring one 6 - - 3 - - 3 - - 3 close,
* Sh2: Ch 6 - - 6, RW,
R 6 - 6 close, (1st ear)
RW, Ch 4, Sh1: R 9 close, Sh2: Ch 4, Sh1: R 9 close, Sh2: Ch 4,

Fig.R2

Fig.R3
RW, place a marker round
Sh1 thread after the last ds.
Sh1: Ch 12 + join to Sh2
thread at the beginning of
the previous chain.
RW, Sh2: Ch 4,
Sh1: R 4 - 2 close,
Sh2: Ch 3 + 5,
Sh1: (with a 4mm picot)
R 2 - - 2 close, RW,
Ch 9, RW,
(to place a bead refer to the
bottom of page 22),
R 2 + b 2 close,
Sh2: Ch 5 - 3,
Sh1: R 2 + 4 close,
Sh2: Ch 4.

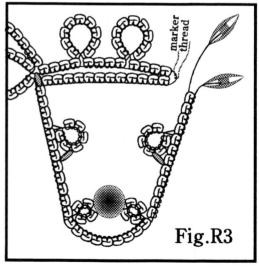

Fig.R3

Fig.R4
Remove the marker and join there
+, RW, R 6 - 6 close (2nd ear), RW, Ch 6 - - 6,
If only one reindeer is being made finish with
Sh1: R 3 - - 3 - - 3 - - 6 close.

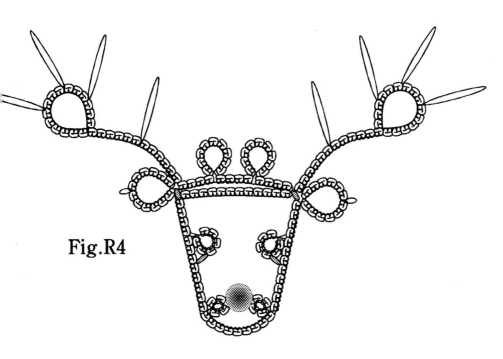

Fig.R4

In an edging (Fig.R5) the reindeer have their antlers crossed so, in place
of the last ring, work:-
Sh1: R 6 - - 3 - - 3 - - 3 close, R 3 - - 3 - - 3 - - 6 close and repeat the pattern
from *.

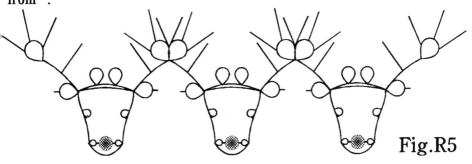

Fig.R5

A single motif could decorate a cracker or other
Christmas novelty. The edging could trim a stocking.

Fir cone wreath

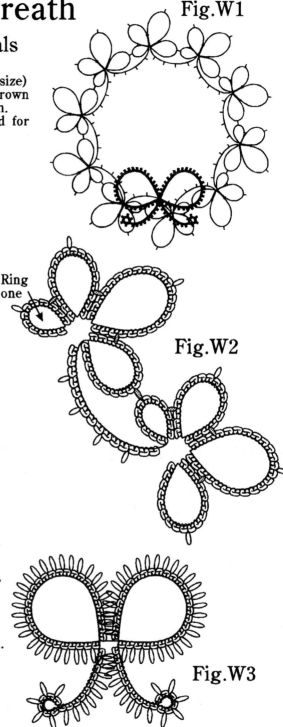

Fig.W1

Suggested materials

DMC Fil a Dentelles No.80
(Fig.W1 will be the approx. size)
Green ball thread and brown
shuttle thread for the wreath.
Red ball and shuttle thread for
the bow.

WREATH Fig.W2
Lengthen all the rings after
closing them by pulling the
middle picot.
Ring one 6 - 3 - 3 close
* R 3 + 6 - 6 - 3 close
R 3 + 9 - 9 - 3 close
R 3 + 6 - 9 close, RW,
Ch 3 - 3 - 3 - 3 - 3, RW,
R 6 + 3 - 3 close,
repeat from * 8 more times
then finish the circle with
R 3 + 6 - 6 - 3 close,
R 3 + 9 - 9 - 3 close,
R 3 + 6 + 9 close, RW,
Ch 3 - 3 - 3 - 3 - 3,
fasten off to the close-up
point of Ring one.
Pin out accurately
(see page 3).

BOW Fig.W3
R (1 -) 5 times, 1 close, RW,
Ch (1 -) 9 times, 1, RW,
R (1 -) 29 times, 1 close,
R (1 -) 29 times, 1 close, RW,
Ch (1 -) 9 times, 1, RW,
R (1 -) 5 times, 1 close.
Fasten off.
Press under a damp cloth
before placing on the wreath.
(Fig.W1)

Ring
one

Fig.W2

Fig.W3

Three Kings
for a Christmas card

When the tatting has been completed wet it and pin into the required shape. When dry place in position on some backing of a suitable colour and texture (larger than the shape shown). Sew all the ends through the backing and use them to hold the pieces in place with some small stitches.

Mount the arrangement in a card with a pre-cut aperture.

Approx. size when worked in DMC Fil a Dentelles No.80

A KING
Sh1: JK 10, RW, Ch 25, RW,
Sh2: Making an 8mm picot Ch 5 - - 5,
the next ring is the head. Twist the 8mm picot twice before joining to it and make the other long picots 4mm.
Sh1: R 7 + 1 - - 1 - 1 - - 1 - 1 - - 8 close
Sh2: Ch 10, Sh1: R 8 close, RW,
Ch 15, RW, JK 10,
Sh2: Ch (2 -) 14 times, 2 ,
fasten off at the start of the first chain.

THE STAR
On these rings make one picot 1cm long and the other three 4mm long.
(R 5 - - 5 close) 4 times.
Tie the ends together.

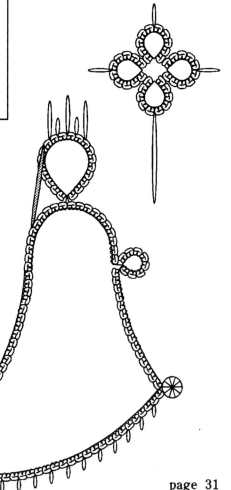

start ⟶

page 31

Bells and Holly
for a Christmas card

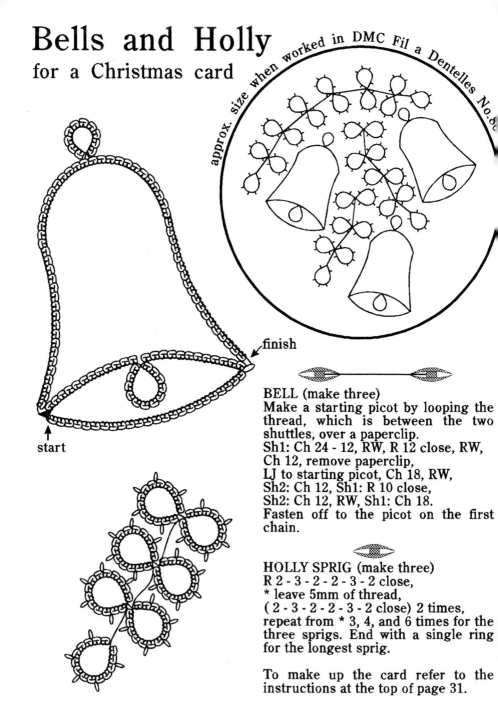

approx. size when worked in DMC Fil a Dentelles No.80

finish

start

BELL (make three)
Make a starting picot by looping the thread, which is between the two shuttles, over a paperclip.
Sh1: Ch 24 - 12, RW, R 12 close, RW,
Ch 12, remove paperclip,
LJ to starting picot, Ch 18, RW,
Sh2: Ch 12, Sh1: R 10 close,
Sh2: Ch 12, RW, Sh1: Ch 18.
Fasten off to the picot on the first chain.

HOLLY SPRIG (make three)
R 2 - 3 - 2 - 2 - 3 - 2 close,
* leave 5mm of thread,
(2 - 3 - 2 - 2 - 3 - 2 close) 2 times,
repeat from * 3, 4, and 6 times for the three sprigs. End with a single ring for the longest sprig.

To make up the card refer to the instructions at the top of page 31.

I have many more Christmas ideas but no room left in the book ..... so look out for 'YULETIDE TATTING 2' !